Transparent Leadership

for Women Who Mean Business

Join the Movement

The World is Waiting…..

Sheri Winesett

Dedication

This book is dedicated to my kids Samantha and Charlie who may at times have mistaken my leadership for bossiness. They are my heart, the next generation of future leaders.

I hope the message and lessons I have shared resonate deeply with Samantha and empower her to continue as the strong and confident leader she is today. And for Charlie, may he always support, practice patience, and honor the unique abilities of the women in his life - those who lead their families and teams while nurturing their empires.

Acknowledgments

First and foremost, I want to thank my husband, Bruce. His unwavering love, acceptance, and belief in me have been my bedrock.

Bruce never hindered my pursuit of growth as a female executive, business owner, and leader of leaders. His respect for my drive and commitment to facilitate change has been unwavering. He pivots alongside me, wherever life takes us. As the best dad, my rock, and my biggest supporter, his patience and selflessness remain unmatched.

Second, I want to extend profound gratitude to all of my clients who have trusted me and confided in me. Without you, there would be no book on transparent leadership.

Table of Contents

Foreword

In a world teeming with noise, where authenticity often takes a backseat to pretense, we find ourselves yearning for leaders who embody the essence of true leadership. The kind of leadership that transcends mere titles and positions, reaching deep into the core of our being, our inner core and outer core. There is more fake in the world today than transparency and openness. We are facing a major lack of leadership at a time when it matters most.

Transparency is not a mere buzzword; it is the bedrock upon which great leaders stand; the cornerstone of trustworthy leadership. Transparency extends beyond teams. Becoming a transparent leader creates a ripple effect having a positive impact on your clients, stakeholders, and the community. When leaders embody the 7 keys that Sheri is going to share with you, they create a legacy of authenticity and impact having created cultures where honesty thrives.

No longer do people yearn for the enigmatic leader; they seek someone who shares the truth, even when it's uncomfortable. Transparent leaders don't hide their vulnerabilities. They admit mistakes, acknowledge uncertainties, and seek input. In doing so, they create an environment where others feel safe to do the same.

When leaders share information transparently, their teams can make informed decisions. Whether it's budget cuts or strategic shifts, transparency empowers individuals to plan their futures. Transparent leadership weaves resilience into the fabric of the company.

Sheri doesn't merely pay lip service to the ideals she's going to share with you; she lives them. In a landscape where smoke and mirrors abound, Sheri's unwavering commitment to transparency shines like a guiding star. She understands that true leadership begins with self-awareness—the ability to see beyond the surface and delve into the depths of one's character.

Her journey has been one of discovery—a quest to unlock the secrets of leadership greatness. She is a seasoned and well-respected executive who has a lot of life experiences that she brings to this book to make the 7 Keys come alive. She's the real deal and someone who has played at a high level.

I first met Sheri in April 2020 when she helped me launch my executive coaching franchise. She is the glue that holds any team together. She puts her heart and soul into anything she builds. Even in times of adversity she always takes the high road and puts her best foot forward. I greatly trust and respect the leader that she was then and that she is today. She is a great leader. I witnessed first-hand her building a team for my company that embodied the 7 keys that she shares in this book.

These seven keys, nestled deep within her core, have been her compass. She's a visionary who sees beyond the horizon, painting a vivid picture of what could be. But her vision isn't confined to dreams—it's grounded in action. She possesses the rare ability of a visionary to turn vision into reality through execution. I have always admired her ability to integrate teams. She can seamlessly integrate strategy, people, and purpose. Her leadership isn't fragmented; it's holistic. Her legacy will ripple through generations, leaving behind a tapestry of authenticity, impact, and inspiration.

So, as you embark on this journey with Sheri to unlock your leadership potential, remember that leadership greatness isn't reserved for the few—it's within your grasp. Let Sheri's 7 Keys ignite the fire within you, and may you, too, become a beacon of authentic leadership and become the leader you can be and must be!

John Mattone, the World's Top Executive Coach
Founder, John Mattone Global, Inc.

A Peek Behind the Curtain

"You are more powerful than you know; you are beautiful just as you are." - Melissa Etheridge, Musician and Activist.

Have you ever felt like you aren't living up to your potential? Are you praying for the secret formula to accelerate your growth and achieve your big professional goals while balancing everything else going on in your life? Have you ever felt like throwing in the towel because you are tired of being needed and pulled in too many directions?   Do you ever feel guilty about wanting more? Stop it! You were meant for greatness, and you can do hard things!

I've seen women give up on their professional goals and put everyone else first because it all seems complicated and overwhelming. They are a mother, a sister, a wife, or a caretaker for an elderly parent and feel guilty for giving one more attention than another. So, what do they give up on? They give up on their dreams for themselves. You don't have to give up on anything, especially your dreams. It's not necessary. Realize that whatever is going on in your life, it's just a season in your life, and you will go through many more seasons. Enduring these seasons and being grateful for them make you a great leader.

Even if you feel like you aren't doing enough, or you hit your limit and think there has got to be something more. That just means you're not fulfilled or you're out of balance. It could be that you're not passionate about what you do and you're not working in your zone of genius. Take a deep breath. It's ok. We all feel this way from time to time. Things change, we change. Embrace the change and say nice things to yourself. We all need help at times realigning to find what fuels us and to help us determine where we want to make an impact. Let the change in seasons bring you a sense of calmness and get you excited for the next season. Commit to being the best you can be so you can shine your light on others no matter the season.

I was once a person who made the following statements. Do any of them resonate with you? "I'm tired of herding cats!" "I'm just plain exhausted," or "This toxic workplace is running me down." Or how about these, "I'm tired of feeling needed," "There isn't enough of me to go around," and "I wish people would just do their job!" While all of these statements seemed authentic, I finally realized my thoughts, my actions, and my choices were making me less powerful than I was meant to be as a leader. I needed help, self-awareness, and a realignment. The great news is that you can create self-awareness, give yourself a check-up from the neck up, and get back on track to be the leader you were meant to be. Never quit trying to become a better version of yourself. You have superpowers that were granted to you and no one else. You are here for a particular reason, and we need you to make an impact on the world.

We need women to level up and stay in the game! Research shows that there are certain traits that women possess that contribute to the effectiveness of women in leading teams: Empathy and emotional intelligence, communication skills, collaborative leadership style, resilience and adaptability, diverse perspectives, empowerment of others, integrity, and ethics. I have observed it, and there are studies out there that prove it. So, why do most women temper their unique abilities to lead instead of unleashing their full potential?

It's all too common to feel imposter syndrome and guilt, causing women to give up on their dreams. No handbook is given to you to unlock your leadership potential when climbing the ladder, seeking significance, and creating impact. You're one of the lucky ones if you have had a strong mentor guiding you on your leadership journey and helping you navigate the waters of also being a rockstar mother, sister, wife, or caretaker for an elderly parent.

The fact is that women have many hats they wear and most do it well even if they feel like they are drowning. I am here to help you see that it is a superpower and show you how to leverage it in your professional career to lead others. Instead of letting all the hats you wear weigh you down, I am going to show you how it lifts you and accelerates your ability to lead.

If you hear others say that achieving success and having it all is difficult, ignore them. That's a victim mindset, and you are a victor. I will teach you how to harness your female superpower that I keep talking about and lead with authenticity, integrity, and transparency to guarantee your success. It will multiply the fun factor and reignite your passion, which will spill into all areas of your life.

This book helps you shift your perspective and enables you to become aware of your limiting beliefs and the limiting beliefs of those around you. It also provides real strategies and tactics that you can implement with your team. If you keep an open mind, get rid of your "I know" attitude, and embrace the Kaizen Principle of constant and never-ending improvement, you will not only be sought out as one of the top five people that others want in their circle, but you will be a leader of champions who will leave a lasting legacy.

I have found it an incredible honor to lead others, and I want you to feel the same. Not only can you be a teacher and mentor to so many, but you can also give people hope and be someone they can trust and depend on. By following this guide to unlocking your leadership potential, you can make an impact and change lives. You have what it takes. You are more powerful than you know.

Being a transparent leader in any business, whether your own or someone else's, is a huge responsibility that can sometimes feel heavy. However, you'll find the rewards extraordinary by learning and executing the seven keys I will share in this book!

When people buy into you as their leader, they will buy into your vision, and you will be able to create the most fantastic culture that others want to be a part of. There will be no struggles with retention, so-so performance, or lack of motivation. Your fire will fuel their fire. Your desire to be the best version of yourself will inspire others to be the best version of themselves and pay it forward.

This book is for female entrepreneurs, business owners, executives, giggers, and side hustlers who want to unlock their leadership potential, do the right thing, and have fun! It's for those who wish to gain massive traction to take themselves, their team, and their business to new heights!

You can show up every day and work with people who think about what's possible, and show up prepared and excited to hit big goals. Have you ever thought about what it would be like for everyone to be as excited to go to work on Monday morning as they were to go to happy hour on Friday night? Amazing, right? Who doesn't want that? We just need some guidance on how to obtain that, and that's what I want to share with you in this book, so you can share it with others.

It starts with you. You are enough. You were born with leadership greatness in you, and I want to help you empower others to achieve their highest potential for maximum impact.

If you've lost your mojo, you can get it back! If you're lacking direction, keep reading. I will show you how you can lead organizations and even countries that deliver a balance between knowledge (the head) and wisdom (the heart). You can become a leader that others can relate to and trust. Just follow my guide to become a Transparent Leader.

The most outstanding leaders are called to serve and are natural problem solvers who are all about the people. Great leaders believe there is no "I" in the team. It's all about Us and not about ME. Great leaders are humble and don't yearn for the pedestal. They are rewarded in ways other than recognition and authority.

I've seen companies fall apart because the leader lacked authenticity. Successful law firms shut down, and equity partners go to jail because of a lack of integrity. Organizations fall apart time and time again because they don't pay attention to the correct numbers in the business or ask the right questions. They lack transparency. These red flags are all indicators of poor leadership. These leadership behaviors negatively impact growth within the organization, displaying a lack of trust, ownership, and accountability, causing any organization to fail or not live up to its potential.

I will guide you down a path to create a lasting legacy that others aspire to be part of while building a culture that produces astronomical results. You can see results in 90 days just by reading this book, committing to executing the seven keys, and breaking free from doing things" the way they have always been done."

In this book, I am going to provide a step-by-step action plan so that:

❖ Challenges are solved much faster. Transparency is a powerful tool that forces a team to work together smarter. It allows everyone to share their perspectives and opinions openly and cultivates an entrepreneurial spirit that allows for cross-functional responsibilities and opportunities.

❖ Work relationships are more authentic. The result: a vibrant and unique team forging powerful relationships because each member is genuine to the other.

❖ Team members trust their leader and are more loyal to the company. A Transparent culture promotes trust at all levels within the team, creating greater connection and loyalty.

❖ The team becomes a high-performing, predictable engine. A culture centered around certainty, contribution, and growth creates a higher-performing company.

People want transparency in leadership. I wrote this book to break the chains of the traditional role of women in leadership, to give seasoned female leaders a new perspective on leadership, and to give aspiring leaders confidence in their ability to lead, the courage to be vulnerable, and the fire to unleash their leadership potential. I want you to be crystal clear on your value as a leader and be able to leverage your unique ability as a female leader in this ever-changing, fast-paced, highly technical world!

Whether you are the CEO, an entrepreneur, a business owner, a seasoned executive, or a stay-at-home mom with a side hustle, this book is for you. I want to show you how to step into your power and be the influential leader the world needs you to be. The next generation and the future of work are depending on us. It's time to unlock your leadership potential. Let's go, girl! You got this! Join the movement. The world is waiting!

Chapter 1

Why You Need to Become a Transparent Leader

"We need women at all levels, including the top, to change the dynamic, reshape the conversation, to make sure women's voices are heard and heeded, not overlooked and ignored." - Sheryl Sandberg

Before you jump into this, I want to tell you who I am and why I am so passionate about helping you shine your light and become a Transparent leader. In this chapter, you will learn how essential leaders and mentors were in my life and how adversity made me the leader I am today. As you read this, I hope you will realize turning points in your life where leaders were present (good and bad) and significantly influenced you. Only then can you understand how significant your influence is on others.

- I believe…… we all have leadership potential. We can all be great leaders if we are willing to create awareness and unlock our unique leadership strengths.
- I believe…. we have a responsibility to lead. The next generation depends on us, and how they lead will reflect how they were led.
- I believe… the closeness of our families, the depths of our relationships, and our well-being depend on our ability to lead with awareness and unwavering purpose.

I am a business owner, business coach, and former franchise executive, passionate about scaling businesses through people. I have helped companies increase their revenue by 46% and profit by 61% by helping leaders level up and coaching high performers to find their moral compass, lead with a big heart, and develop a solid conviction to do the right thing. I've worked with many companies worldwide, from brand-new start-ups and small to medium-sized businesses to nonprofit organizations, government agencies, and large multinationals. I've coached over one thousand entrepreneurs, CEOs, executives, and their teams, some who were great leaders and others who were terrible. I have had the opportunity to observe what it takes to become someone that others want to follow.

My friends and colleagues describe me as driven, fun, intelligent, and loyal.   Looking back now, I can see where those seeds were planted when I was growing up. I was a Navy brat and was surrounded by high achievers. I had role models such as Admirals and Captains who were driven, in command, and loyal to God, country, and family. They had a high level of integrity and a tremendous amount of responsibility.   My mom was a nurse who devoted her entire life to the church, putting God first and caring for others. Her loyalty to faith and family never wavered, nor has her strength to lead our family and adapt to ever-changing circumstances and adversity throughout our military life.   My parents taught me to embrace change by moving to new countries or cities with my eyes open, ready to learn and immerse myself in the following new adventure. We met many new friends and had unique experiences, and with their guidance, I learned to be curious. They also taught me how to have fun. They were outgoing and always had a lot of friends. They were all about the people and were admirable servant leaders.

When I graduated high school, I had no idea what I would be when I grew up. I attended college and was inspired by my college professor to pursue a degree in Political Science. His high passion and high energy garnered the full attention of 200 college students not even in their twenties. He was in his zone of genius and had gained my respect and trust. This professor, who happened to be a former member of the U.S. House of Representatives, was a great storyteller and his leadership and enthusiasm changed the trajectory of my life! He was likable and authentic, and I trusted him. He left a lasting impression on everyone he came in contact with. That is what leaders do. As I reflect on that time, my biggest takeaway is that I bought into him as a respected leader before I ever bought into the vision of becoming a lobbyist.

After college, I worked on Capitol Hill in Washington, D.C. for about a year. Then, I accepted a position off the hill with a prominent Chicago lobbying firm as their Director of Legislative Affairs. In my mid-twenties, I started leading my first team and was introduced to my first mentor. She was a female powerhouse in the legislative world. She was a master at networking, so I quickly became a member of several women's networking organizations, where I volunteered to chair committees, mentor college students, serve on boards, and lead the organization's strategic planning retreats. I went all in and what I remember most about that time was that I had incredible female mentors who I still keep in touch with today.

During my tenure as an international lobbyist, I worked with Fortune 100 C-Suite executives at my law firm, flying first class with my best friend and colleague, sipping Dom Perrigonne and eating lobster bisque, visiting client sites, and lobbying foreign governments. I was even invited to serve on the US Ambassador team to Italy for the next Administration. I was driven, climbing the ladder and leading a talented team. Doors were opening that I had never even imagined.

Life was good... until the bottom dropped out. It was all due to our leadership's lack of integrity and transparency. Our "leader" was arrested and disbarred, and in the blink of an eye, our practice was closed. One person's lack of judgment derailed an entire team's future. Families' lives were disrupted and spouses' paychecks were abruptly taken away because one person didn't do the right thing.

I was at a crossroads. I had a 7-month-old child at home, and my husband and I had plans to expand our family. I could go to another firm working for someone else and climb to the top again while living out of my suitcase and traveling the world, start my own legislative consulting business and be in the same boat, or break free from corporate America and become a business owner. I chose the latter and changed my narrative. Never again would I be in a situation where I was surrounded by leaders making selfish choices that negatively impacted their team. I was disheartened by the lack of integrity, authenticity, transparency, and accountability that I had experienced. I decided to run my race where I could do the right thing, take ownership and accountability for my decisions, and be surrounded by others doing the same.

For the next ten years, I ran my business coaching franchise and received several certifications as a business coach, executive coach, and leadership coach. I eventually partnered up and grew my firm to 100 coaches through acquisitions and mergers. We were the largest business and executive coaching firm in the U.S. I was on top of the world and proud of our team, which made a difference in the lives of business owners and their families. Our business coaches led with integrity and were committed to continuous improvement. They worked to better themselves and taught our clients ownership, accountability, and responsibility in business.

Then things changed. There suddenly became a need for more transparency within the partnership, resulting in a lack of accountability and alignment among the leadership team. As a result, our team of coaches became disenfranchised. I couldn't believe it was happening again. Another group of leaders led without transparency and accountability which caused the partnership to fall apart. The team of coaches are the ones who suffered. They trusted us as their leaders to be in alignment, and we failed them. They deserved better.

Eventually, I sold my shares and launched my independent consulting business. Soon after my departure, the firm fell apart. I went on to serve my clients as a business growth strategist. I vowed to be different and committed to transparency within and outside my organization. I ran my independent consulting business for about five years, and then

COVID hit. You may already be thinking, oh yeah, here comes the sob story, but that's not what's coming at all.

Amazingly, I was recruited by two leaders in the executive coaching space to launch their start-up. They were visionaries and legends in their own right. As CEO, I was to recruit talent, lead the team, and launch the brand. We gained significant traction in our first two years of business, generating 1.2 million in revenue in the first seven months of launching. Keep in mind, we launched in April of 2020, right when COVID hit.

Upon reflection, that was the best team of high performers I have ever had the privilege to lead. That team lived and breathed the 7 Keys of Transparent leadership. We trusted each other; we relied on each other. We constantly improved, took ownership, accountability, and responsibility for our roles within the organization, and we had massive awareness of how our actions or lack of action impacted others within the system. We were collaborators in complete alignment, ready to change the world. We were on fire! Our momentum was off the charts until it wasn't.

Around year two, the lack of trust, alignment, and vision among the founders brought the organization to its knees. The biggest lesson learned is that you can have a great business model and a top-notch team, but a lack of alignment, vision, and trust among senior decision-makers will destroy any great business.

The number one, hands down, biggest challenge I have uncovered working with businesses is a lack of transparency, which leads to toxicity. This has led me to develop the seven keys I am going to share with you in this book. I am going to help you get crystal clear on these seven essential keys and teach you how to wipe out toxicity in any organization by creating transparency in leadership.

I have no regrets, and neither should you! I am grateful for every experience that has led me to where I am today. I am exactly where I am supposed to be, and so are you! These experiences have inspired me to write this book and pay it forward.

This guide was created from real-life examples of businesses and leaders I have personally helped transform their businesses and their lives. You can have the best systems in place, the most cutting-edge software, innovative products, and a great team, but you can only achieve peak performance with outstanding leadership and transparency.

I continue to coach CEOs and their executive teams today. Companies engage me to uncover the issues in their organizations holding them back and present them with a path to take their business and leadership to the next level. My clients who have achieved the best results in record time are women in leadership roles.

We need more women leading at their highest potential. Someone's daughter is watching and modeling you, and you don't even know it, but your impact is profound. She needs to know that she, too, can be a leader of people and not be viewed as bossy, too independent, or an overachiever. College graduates are entering the workforce in droves and seeking transparency, mentorship, and open communication. They will soon experience their first impression of working within a team and being led by a leader, an impression that will last a lifetime. How they are led today is how they will lead in the future.

I promise that if you become a transparent leader and teach others to do the same, you will create transparent cultures and legacies that will last for generations and continue to teach others how to win in business and life!!

So, let's get to work, and together, we can change the world!

Chapter 2

What is Transparent Leadership and Why Does It Matter?

"Leadership is about the team - the culture they keep and embrace, it's about empathy for your customers, clients, employees and the communities where you do business, it's about doing the right thing for the right reasons, being confident enough to take risks and responsible enough to think of those who your decisions and risks may affect." - - Kat Cole (COO & President of FOCUS Brands)

Transparent leadership is characterized by transparency, openness, and authenticity in communication, decision-making, and actions. Transparent leaders do not hide information or operate with hidden agendas but instead foster trust, accountability, and collaboration by providing visibility into their thought processes and actions.

People want leaders who can deliver a balance between knowledge (the head) and wisdom (the heart). More importantly, they want to follow leaders they can relate to and trust, leaders who are congruent and lead with integrity. Being a transparent leader means being a boss who is authentic, with no surprises, and one who does the right thing. Companies that adopt a transparent leadership culture find that challenges are solved much faster.

Transparent leaders can lead great companies and achieve great results because, over time, they build solid relationships based on the seven keys that help them unlock their leadership potential. They are reliable, predictable, and committed to serving and supporting their team. They are trusted and easy to follow, allowing them to achieve their goals, if not change the world.

There are seven essential keys of a Transparent Leader.

Key One...360-degree Accountability & Awareness: Holding yourself and others accountable by taking responsibility for one's actions, decisions, and outcomes and ensuring accountability throughout the organization.

Key Two...Integrity: Honesty, sincerity, upholding moral principles in actions and decisions, and being authentic. A leader with integrity operates ethically, follows through on commitments, and is fair, trustworthy, and consistent.

Key Three...Transparency: Openness, clarity, and accessibility in communication and decision-making. A transparent leader shares information openly, provides reasons behind decisions, and encourages dialogue and feedback, fostering trust and understanding within the organization.

Key Four...Vision: A clear, inspiring, forward-looking perspective of the future direction and goals. A leader with vision communicates a compelling vision to their team, inspires commitment and alignment towards common objectives, and navigates the team towards a desired future state.

Key Five...Congruence: Alignment and consistency between a leader's words, actions, and values. A congruent leader behaves authentically, practicing what they preach and ensuring alignment between organizational values, goals, and actions.

Key Six...Alignment: Ensuring that individuals' and teams' actions, goals, and efforts are coordinated and synchronized toward common objectives. A leader fosters alignment by clearly communicating expectations, providing direction, and facilitating collaboration and teamwork.

Key Seven...Measurement: Systematic assessment and evaluation of progress towards goals and objectives. A leader uses relevant metrics, key performance indicators (KPIs), and feedback mechanisms to track performance, identify areas for improvement, and make informed decisions to drive success.

Transparent leadership matters for several reasons:

1. Building Trust: Transparency breeds trust. When leaders are transparent about their intentions, decisions, and actions, trust among their team, customers, and stakeholders is fostered. Trust is essential for building relationships and promoting a culture that others are proud to be part of.

2. Enhancing Accountability: Transparent leaders hold themselves and others accountable for their actions and decisions. By being open about their performance and accepting responsibility for mistakes, transparent leaders set an example for accountability within the organization.

3. Promoting Collaboration: Transparent leadership encourages open communication and collaboration. When leaders share information openly and invite input from the team and

stakeholders, it creates a culture of collaboration where diverse perspectives are valued and considered in decision-making processes.

4. Increasing Engagement: Transparent leaders engage their team by giving them visibility into the organization's goals, strategies, and performance. When your team understands how they contribute to the broader objective, they feel more engaged and motivated to contribute their best efforts.

5. Facilitating Problem-Solving: Transparent leadership enables effective problem-solving. When leaders are transparent about the organization's challenges and opportunities, their team and stakeholders can brainstorm solutions collaboratively and work towards common goals.

6. Improving Decision-Making: Transparency leads to better decision-making. When leaders share information openly and involve stakeholders in decision-making, it ensures that decisions are well-informed and aligned with the values and objectives of the organization.

7. Enhancing Reputation: Transparent leadership enhances your reputation. When leaders are transparent about their actions and decisions, it builds credibility and integrity, which are vital for maintaining a positive reputation in the eyes of team members, customers, and the broader community.

Transparent leadership fosters a culture of trust, accountability, collaboration, and engagement within organizations. By being transparent, leaders can inspire confidence, drive performance, and positively impact overall success.

Key characteristics of a transparent culture include:

1. Open Communication: In a transparent culture, communication flows and leaders are accessible. Leaders share information freely, and team members feel comfortable asking questions, providing feedback, and expressing their opinions.

2. Honesty and Integrity: Transparency is built on honesty and integrity. Leaders are truthful and

forthright in their communication and adhere to ethical standards in all aspects of their decision-making and actions.

3. Visibility into Decision-Making: The team has visibility into the decision-making processes within the organization. Leaders explain the rationale behind decisions and involve the team in discussions about important issues that affect them.

4. Accessible Leadership: In a transparent culture, leaders are approachable and available to answer questions, address concerns, and engage in open dialogue with anyone on the team.

5. Feedback and Accountability: A transparent culture encourages and values feedback. Regular feedback on performance is given, and leaders are receptive to feedback from their team. Accountability is emphasized, and individuals are responsible for their actions and decisions.

6. Information Sharing: Information is shared openly and proactively. Team members can easily access relevant information about the organization's goals, strategies, financial performance, and other vital metrics.

7. Trust and Respect: Transparency fosters trust and respect. When information is shared openly and communication is honest, it builds confidence in leadership and strengthens relationships within the organization.

A transparent culture promotes trust, collaboration, and engagement within an organization.

Team members feel like their voices matter. Whether sharing feedback on a new project or expressing concerns about a company decision, they know their opinions are valued and heard by leadership. This level of openness transforms an individual's perspective on work. People are empowered knowing that their contributions make a difference.

Transparent leadership can profoundly impact your team's morale and productivity. When everyone has access to the same information and understands the reasoning behind decisions, it eliminates confusion and creates a sense of unity. I've seen firsthand how transparency leads to greater trust among team members and ultimately drives better results. I have also seen co-workers put a tremendous amount of emphasis on accountability and show appreciation for leaders who don't just talk the talk but walk the walk. If a mistake is made, they own up to it and work with their team to find a solution. It creates a culture where everyone feels safe taking risks and learning from failures, knowing they have their leaders' support every step of the way.

These are just some positive benefits you can expect from being a Transparent leader who develops a transparent culture.

Can you imagine?

Chapter 3

Leading with 360 Degrees of Accountability & Awareness

It's okay to admit what you don't know. It's okay to ask for help. And it's more than okay to listen to the people you lead- in fact, it's essential." - Mary Barra, CEO General Motors

Key One...360-degree Accountability: Holding yourself and others accountable by taking responsibility for one's actions, decisions, and outcomes and ensuring accountability throughout the organization.

Are you seeing attrition, bad behavior, lack of drive, and procrastination among your team? If you don't like what you see in your team, look in the mirror.

The first key to becoming a Transparent leader is a 360-degree view of your actions, decisions, and outcomes which involves a deep dive into your self-awareness. This first step can take you out of your comfort zone, which is precisely why you must do it. When we get uncomfortable, we have breakthroughs and self-discovery. What distinguishes average leaders from rock star leaders is their willingness to get out of their comfort zone, get rid of their I Know and ask for help. Some people call this being vulnerable.

Many leaders need to take the time to develop awareness of their strengths and behaviors in and out of the office. When things aren't going your way, do you point the finger at someone else? Have you noticed that when someone points a finger at someone else, more fingers point back at them? Try it. This is not a coincidence. The best leaders understand their strengths and their shortsightedness. They also admit where they fall short and work on improving their behaviors and up-leveling their skills.

And remember, you're not just a leader at work. You may be the leader of your family; you may be a leader of your church, a leader among your network and your friends, or a leader of leaders! How you show up as a leader at work is how you show up everywhere! There does not need to be a separation of business and personal behaviors. You can do all the assessments you want, but to be the best leader you can be, you must work to be as natural in the workplace as you are at home. Strive to be even keel. What people see in you is what they should see in you all the time. This is what we call your authentic self.

Here are some action steps you can take right away to build your self-awareness.

Do a Checkup from the Neck Up Daily.

How's your thinking?

Do you have stinking thinking?

What are you doing to evaluate how you show up as a leader daily in all areas of your life? How's your financial health? How is your physical health? How's your spiritual health? Family health? Do you have awareness in all of these areas in your life? It seems like a lot to think about. Still, if you wrote the following questions on a sticky pad in your notebook or keyed them into your calendar invite as a daily reminder, you can be mindful of all the areas in your life that impact your thinking and well-being. Mindfulness is the first step to greatness. Be conscious at the beginning of every day.

Gain outside perspectives.

It's helpful to gain some outside perspectives as well, and below are some simple ways to do it. Without outside perspectives you are not able to become aware of your blindspots. What prevents us from taking action is our fear of being vulnerable. Overcome it! Be curious! Taking action on one of these will provide incredible insight to set you on a path to becoming your best self!

1. Just ask! Go on social media and ask your friends and followers to comment with three words that describe you. It's essential to understand how others perceive you. Let the feedback tell you where you shine and get you aligned and operating within your zone of genius.

2. Take an Assessment - Do a 360 leadership assessment, strengths finder, DISC behavior profile, the Kolbe index, or one of the many other assessment tools. Find out how you communicate and like to be communicated with, understand how you approach situations and tackle projects, gain perspective on your strengths, and leverage them. Be vulnerable and let others share how they see you as a leader.

   If you have already taken several assessments, when was the last time you reviewed them? Assessments are like strategic plans; most people put them on the shelf and don't use them as tools to guide them down the path to success. I have had so many clients say, "It's so interesting!", "I can't believe they nailed it with 20 questions!" "It's freakishly me!" and on and on.

The real power of these assessments and what will separate you from others who take them is not the confirmation of who you are but how you use them to lead others. Taking the assessment and reading the reports is the easy part. Take the feedback and take action!

3. <u>Be Aware of Your Triggers</u>. Triggers are those little things that set you off in a big way. They usually produce some sort of emotion or feeling. Whether it's fear, anger, hesitancy…, or whatever it is, determine how to manage your reaction to it and get to the root of why it's triggering you.

I recently worked with a coach to help me with unprocessed emotions. What I found is there were certain things I was holding on to in my past that were triggering anxiety or anger in me, and it didn't matter why. Seriously, it didn't matter why they were triggering me. What mattered was that I gained self-awareness around those moments. When you get angry, for example, that moment is the perfect time to catch yourself, take a deep breath, and ask yourself what made you angry and why. Dig deep. What's it really about?

Here's an example of a trigger. I got super mad at my dog for eating one of my pillows. He's a puppy. He's nine months old. He's innocent. He only wanted to please me, but I took it so personally. I felt disrespected. And so, why was I feeling so disrespected? What was essential for me was having awareness around it, and by digging deeper and asking myself why, I realized it had nothing to do with my sweet dog eating my pillow. It wasn't about the dog; it was about how the dog made me feel, and that feeling came from an unprocessed emotion based on an experience from my past. Be aware of your feelings because they appear as emotions on the outside. It may sound confusing, but it took a massive weight off my shoulders to eliminate negative emotions I didn't even know were present. So, if you are intrigued or want some help with this, pick up the book Self Sabotage No More by Jennie Potter.

Remove the excuses

Excuses create scarce thoughts, resulting in self-doubt. They are always a recipe for disaster, and if you listen and observe closely, you'll realize that people have started to believe their excuses. Excuses are all around us and are a form of avoidance behavior that conveys a lack of ownership and accountability, possibly due to a lack of confidence, knowledge, and a handful of other emotions or traits. When we make up excuses for not doing the right thing or doing what we said we would do, we don't get to the root of the issue and solve the problem to prevent the behavior from happening again. It's a never-ending cycle. The excuses that you tell yourself and others will impact the belief system of generations to come. That's a pretty big cross to bear when you think of it that way, isn't it? So, let's eliminate our excuses and live up to our full potential.

Below are the four most common excuses I hear from the powerhouse women I coach with. Yes, you read that right. They are powerhouses in their industry, and they even have excuses that get in the way of them progressing towards their goals.

Excuse #1—It should be easier. When you say it should be easier, ask yourself what you want to be easier. What could have made it easier? What is one thing within your power that you could do or change to make it easier? Taking the time to ask yourself these questions empowers you to shift your paradigm and puts you in problem-solving mode.

Excuse #2: I don't have enough time. Time is your most significant resource. We all have the same amount of time, yet most people never have enough time. Doesn't that sound unbelievable? Ask yourself, where am I spending my time? How could I utilize my time better? What do I need to stop doing? What do I need to start doing?

No matter how you slice it, there are 24 hours in a day. If it's important enough to you, you will prioritize your time. Just recognize that sometimes it's about something other than having more resources but prioritizing your time utilizing your resources.

Excuse #3: I don't have enough resources. Ask yourself what you are doing with the resources you do have. Are you spending time maximizing them, or are you thinking about what you don't have, allowing it to become a distraction and prevent you from moving forward?

Excuse #4: I have no quality of life—Your quality of life is determined by your choices and how you react to situations. While it's understandable to feel overwhelmed or dissatisfied at times, it's important to recognize that quality of life is not solely determined by external circumstances but also by our mindset and how we respond to our circumstances.

You can influence and shape your environment, professionally and personally. You have the power to say no. You choose the people you hang out with, the books you read, and the shows you watch. You can design your life and prioritize yourself! Then, you will shift from feeling powerless to being powerful and unstoppable.

Leadership involves recognizing challenges as opportunities for growth and improvement. By taking proactive steps to address issues, you can enhance your quality of life and those around you. This includes setting boundaries, prioritizing self-care, and cultivating a healthy work-life balance.

Accountability also plays a crucial role in maintaining and improving quality of life. By holding yourself accountable for your actions, decisions, and well-being, you empower yourself to make positive changes and overcome obstacles.

Excuse #5 - I can't do XXX because no one is buying into my vision - Are you focused on the people? Win the people and win the race. People have to buy into you before they buy into your vision. When you become a Transparent leader, you will create raving fans that will become your brand champions. When you become a Transparent Leader, you will find that a compelling vision grows its wings.

Be Aware of Your Leadership Style and That of Others

Leadership styles and approaches can vary significantly. The best leaders understand not only their own but, more importantly, the leadership styles of others. Remember, it's all about the people. Once you understand how others operate, you can move mountains and adapt your leadership style to achieve the results you are seeking, creating win-win situations.

Women are born with an innate ability to adapt.   I am often asked what the magic bullet is for achieving my true leadership potential.   The answer? Staying focused on what you can control. You can't control how others behave, but you can 100% control your behaviors and adapt your leadership to achieve the most effective and impactful outcomes from others.

Be grateful for your mistakes.

Admitting mistakes and learning from them is a sign of strength, not weakness. Establish a culture where mistakes are viewed as growth opportunities and learning from failure is celebrated. Teach your team to be grateful for their mistakes and help them understand there is no such thing as failure.   You either win or learn. What mistake have you made that has become one of your biggest lessons? Share it with someone else and celebrate it! By being vulnerable, you can help the person you used to be!

Chapter 4

Leading with Integrity: Cultivating Trust

*"Real integrity is doing the right thing, knowing that nobody's going to know whether you did it or not." -
Oprah Winfrey*

Key Two... Integrity encompasses honesty, sincerity, and upholding moral principles in one's actions and decisions. A leader with integrity operates ethically, follows through on commitments, and is fair, trustworthy, and consistent.

People want to be led by someone who shows compassion and tells the truth.   Someone they can relate to and trust. A transparent boss with no surprises.

Imagine how you would feel if your culture operated and made decisions based on Doing the

Right Thing. One of my client's core values is "Do the Right Thing." It attracted me to his organization. What was mind-blowing is that he stood firm in upholding this moral principle. He led with integrity and established incredible loyalty from his customers and team. What are your moral principles? Have you shared them with your team? If you asked your team to list your company's or team's core values, how many would be able to list them all? You have some work to do if the answer is not 100%.

Integrity matters. It forms the foundation of trust, credibility, ethical decision-making, strong relationships, effective leadership, personal fulfillment, and societal well-being. It is a core value that guides individuals in living authentically and positively, contributing to the world around them. It is rated highly as a core value among teams because it instills professionalism, collaboration, engagement, retention, and loyalty. Organizations that prioritize integrity create a positive work environment and attract and retain top talent, leading to long-term success.

People want to work for somebody that they like, somebody they trust, and someone with values they can align with. That's how you gain their respect; you let them know what you are about. They know what's important to you. Once you communicate and act on your values, you will attract a team with similar values that will walk the walk with you. Together, you will be able to build a cohesive unit that not only respects but lives out those values.

You gain respect from those you are leading when you do what you say and are willing to do what you ask of others. Lead people down a path to success that they feel good about, and you will become a leader that people want to follow instead of a leader they have been told to follow or feel compelled to obey. Your team will mirror what you do. Gone are the days of doing what I say and not as I do. You must earn the right to lead others.

Great leaders have a no-tolerance rule for someone who lacks integrity. When you spot someone on your team lacking integrity, remove them. Hold them accountable for their actions, and do not try to make them someone they are not. Unfortunately, more times than not, I have seen companies hold on to team members way too long who do not align with their values and it sets them back years, disrupting the culture and creating unnecessary drama within the organization.

When teams are focused on dealing with ethical dilemmas, navigating conflicts, or questioning leaders' motives, it can detract from their ability to focus on their work and achieve their goals. Enough is enough! Act quickly; you will be light years ahead instead of light years behind. A team that values honesty, fairness, and ethical behavior will likely seek another home if they perceive a lack of integrity within the organization.

Take time to reflect on your core values and moral principles. Determine where you stand as a leader and how you communicate those principles to your team. Engage your team in discussions about values and aspirations. Leaders must be respected to effectively lead others.

Great leaders are able to answer the following questions:

1. How will I communicate my core values and principles with my team?
2. Which core value resonates most with my team, and why is it important to them?
3. How will I recognize people on my team for failing fast?

Chapter 5

Embracing Transparency: A Cornerstone for Effective Leadership

In the absence of transparency, suspicion thrives. - Unknown

Key Three...Transparency: Openness, clarity, and accessibility in communication and decision-making. A transparent leader shares information openly, provides reasons behind decisions, and encourages dialogue and feedback, fostering trust and understanding within the organization.

Transparency is not just a buzzword but a fundamental principle underpinning successful leadership. In leadership, transparency means opening up, showing vulnerability, and being authentic with those you lead. It's about establishing an environment of trust where honesty and openness prevail. In this chapter, we dive into the importance of transparency in leadership and how it can shape culture, foster confidence, and drive success.

As a leader, showing your true self to your team members is essential. How do you show up? Are you genuine, honest, and vulnerable? When you open up about your experiences, values, and beliefs, you create a deeper connection with your team. You show them you're not just a figurehead but a human being with flaws, insecurities, and aspirations. By sharing your authentic self, you invite others to do the same, creating a culture of openness and trust.

Moreover, transparency involves giving credit where it's due. Openly and publicly acknowledge your team members' contributions, celebrate their successes and achievements, and show appreciation for their hard work and dedication. When you shine a spotlight on others, you boost morale and motivation and build a culture of collaboration and support.

Be humble. Admit when you've fallen short. You're not infallible as a leader, and pretending otherwise only undermines your credibility. Instead, accept your mistakes, take responsibility, and learn from them. By demonstrating humility and a willingness to learn and grow, you set a powerful example for your team. You show them it's okay to make mistakes if you're willing to own up to them and strive to improve.

Transparency isn't just about sharing information; it's about sharing your thoughts, feelings, and experiences openly and honestly. It's about letting others see behind the curtain and understand the motivations and reasons behind your actions. When you're transparent with your team, you empower them to understand the bigger picture and make informed decisions. You give them insight into your thought process and invite them to contribute their ideas and perspectives. In doing so, you encourage a culture of collaboration and innovation where everyone feels valued and empowered to make a difference.

Vulnerability is a crucial aspect of transparency allowing you to be open about your vulnerabilities, fears, and insecurities. Many leaders fear vulnerability, believing it will make them appear weak or incompetent. However, vulnerability is a strength, not a weakness. When you're vulnerable with your team, you show them it's okay to be imperfect and have doubts and uncertainties. You create a safe space where people feel comfortable expressing themselves and taking risks. This builds trust and camaraderie, as people feel connected to you on a deeper level.

Let me share a personal anecdote to illustrate the importance of transparency in leadership. In a previous role, I encountered a colleague who lacked transparency. They made decisions behind closed doors without consulting or informing their team members. As a result, the team had a pervasive sense of distrust and uncertainty. People felt left in the dark, unsure where the organization was headed or how their roles fit into the bigger picture. Morale suffered, and productivity declined as a result. The company shut down 2.5 years after it started.

Being a leader is not just about sharing the good; be open about the bad. When problems arise, it's essential to address them openly and transparently. It humanizes you as a leader. This requires humility and courage, which may mean admitting fault or acknowledging shortcomings. However, it's essential for building trust and maintaining credibility. By owning up to mistakes and addressing them openly, you demonstrate integrity and a commitment to accountability. Moreover, you create an environment where forgiveness and growth are possible. Instead of sweeping problems under the rug or blaming others, transparency allows you to confront issues head-on and work towards solutions collaboratively.

Keep your team informed about important decisions, changes, and developments. Create an environment where questions and concerns are welcomed and addressed promptly. Lead by example, demonstrating transparency in your actions and behaviors. Be open about your thought process, decision-making criteria, and challenges you face. Show vulnerability when appropriate and invite feedback from others.

Encourage feedback and input by creating opportunities for dialogue and collaboration within your team. Create feedback loops and encourage team members to openly share their ideas, concerns, and perspectives. Actively listen to their feedback and consider it when making decisions.

Be crystal clear about your expectations, goals, and values. Show appreciation for your team members' contributions and celebrate their successes. And for the love of all that is good, address problems openly and transparently immediately when problems arise. Avoid sweeping issues under the rug or ignoring them, in hopes that the problem will magically disappear. Instead, confront them head-on and work towards solutions collaboratively.

It may make you uncomfortable but it is essential for effective leadership. By being open, honest, and authentic with your team, you foster trust, collaboration, and innovation. Embrace transparency as a core value of your leadership style, and you'll create a culture where everyone feels valued, empowered, and motivated to succeed.

Chapter 6

Visionary Leadership: Fostering Passion, Significance, and Clarity

"Leadership is hard to define, and good leadership even harder. But if you can get people to follow you to the ends of the earth, you are a great leader." - Indra Nooyi (Former CEO, PepsiCo)

Key Four...Vision: A clear, inspiring, and forward-looking perspective of the future direction and goals of the organization. A leader with vision communicates a compelling vision to their team, inspires commitment and alignment towards common objectives, and navigates the organization towards its desired future state.

First things first....You have to sell yourself before you sell your vision. Once people buy into

YOU as their leader, they will buy into the vision. They buy into you when you show up, take the lead, and get the result. Remember, you make the difference, not the vision.

Gaining buy-in for your vision can often take time and effort, primarily if the vision represents change. However, a clear and compelling vision communicated by a respected leader grows its wings.

Once you have won the people over, clear, compelling and constant communication will help you maintain buy-in for the vision. Many leaders can clearly articulate their vision but fall short in communicating the benefits and impact that achieving the vision will have on the team, the stakeholders and the rest of the world! People are more likely to lock arms with a vision that resonates with their beliefs and goals. Consider whether your vision aligns with the values, needs, and priorities of those you're trying to engage. Take the time to listen to others' perspectives and tailor your message to address their concerns and motivations.

Demonstrate your commitment to the vision through your actions and decisions, and be patient as others see its value. Small wins or tangible progress toward the vision can help garner support and create traction but it may take time. Great leaders stay the course and realize it is not a one and done approach. Find your brand champions and raving fans. Collaborate with them to leverage their influence to help spread the word and gain influence.

By focusing on clarity, alignment, trust-building, and collaboration, you can work towards gaining the support and enthusiasm needed to bring your vision to life. You have to be willing to stay the course. You want your vision to be a guiding light, inspiring and motivating your team to strive for greatness.

The Power of Passion

Passion is critical to achieving buy-in for your vision. Passion fuels conviction making you contagious and irresistible to follow. It produces energy and stimulates creativity. You can fuel other people's fire when your heart is on fire. I have always told my clients if I can catch their vision, I will be their biggest brand champion.

If you struggle to articulate the big picture, you can use tools like the Business Model Canvas to explain where you are headed. Since your business model describes the rationale of how your organization creates, delivers, and captures value, it just makes sense to use the model for others who need to see what's possible. The model is a game-changer and has typically been used by startups to scale quickly, allowing them to establish, test, and prove a business model before launching. However, it is also an effective tool for communication, taking into account visual, auditory, and kinesthetic learners. Sometimes, you must show how all the pieces fit together to gain buy-in for your vision.

The canvas is one of the most effective tools for my visionary clients who need assistance in communicating in more detail. It provides a structured framework for articulating the components that will help achieve the vision in concrete terms. By breaking down your business model into its constituent parts, you can effectively communicate the value you aim to create, how you plan to deliver it, and how you will capture value in return. This helps your team members understand the big picture and empowers them to align their efforts with the overall vision and strategy.

The tool facilitates communication across different learning styles allowing visual learners to grasp the concept by seeing the business components of the canvas, auditory learners can engage in discussions and hear your presentation about each building block, and kinesthetic learners can participate in hands-on activities such as brainstorming sessions and workshops that allow them to document the process to get there. This multi-dimensional approach ensures that your vision resonates with every team member, regardless of their preferred learning style.

To learn more, you can go online and download your copy of the Business Model Canvas or order a copy of the Business Model Generation book by Alexander Osterwalder and Yves Pigneur.

In addition to using the Business Model Canvas, there are several other strategies and tactics you can employ to articulate and communicate your vision effectively:

1. Storytelling: Craft compelling narratives that bring your vision to life. Use storytelling techniques to illustrate its potential impact. Personal anecdotes, case studies, and examples can make your vision more relatable and memorable.

2. Visual Aids: Use visual aids such as charts, graphs, and diagrams to illustrate key concepts and ideas. Visual representations can simplify complex

information and help your team members understand and internalize your vision.

3. Engage Stakeholders: Involve key stakeholders in the visioning process. Seek input and feedback from customers and trusted partners to ensure your vision resonates with their needs and aspirations. By involving stakeholders in the process, you create a sense of ownership and buy-in that is essential for success.

4. Lead by Example: Demonstrate your commitment to the vision through your actions and behaviors. Be a role model for your team members, embodying the values and principles that underpin your vision. Your authenticity and passion will inspire others to rally behind the vision and work towards its realization.

5. Communicate Consistently: Regularly communicate updates and progress toward the vision. Keep your team members informed about milestones, achievements, and challenges at

weekly meetings. Start every meeting by stating the vision. Transparent and consistent communication builds trust and keeps everyone aligned with the organization's vision and goals.

Articulating and communicating your vision is a critical aspect of leadership. Leveraging tools like the Business Model Canvas and employing effective communication strategies can inspire and motivate your team to work towards a shared vision of success.

Remember, passion fuels energy, and significance encourages greatness. By sharing your vision with clarity and conviction, you can ignite your team members' passion and purpose, driving them to achieve extraordinary results.

Chapter 7

The Power of Congruency: Aligning Your Words, Actions, and Values

"If your actions create a legacy that inspires others to dream more, learn more, do more and become more, then, you are an excellent leader." -Dolly Parton

Key Five...Congruence: Alignment and consistency between a leader's words, actions, and values. A congruent leader behaves authentically, practicing what they preach and ensuring alignment between organizational values, goals, and actions.

Being congruent means being true to oneself and in sync with one's values, beliefs, and attitudes. It is a state of consistency between what one says and what one does. The way one thinks and feels should also be the way one behaves. Being incongruent can lead to mistrust and a lack of credibility.

Being congruent can be challenging. It requires self-awareness, honesty, and integrity. It means understanding who you are and what is important to you. It means doing the right thing, even when difficult or unpopular. It means being accountable for your actions and taking responsibility for your mistakes.

Incongruence, on the other hand, can have negative consequences. It can lead to mistrust and a lack of respect, as well as internal conflict and a sense of dissonance.

To be congruent, you must be transparent and authentic. You must be willing to stand up for what you believe in, even when it is difficult, and do the right thing, even when it is unpopular.

Congruence helps you gain credibility while incongruence leads to mistrust and a lack of credibility. Here are some tips to help you become more congruent:

1. Define your values: Identify what is important to you and what you stand for. Write down your values and beliefs and ensure they align with your actions.

2. Practice self-reflection: Reflect on your thoughts, feelings, and actions. Ask yourself if you are true to your values and if your actions align with your words.

3. Be accountable: Take responsibility for your actions and mistakes. Admit when you are wrong and make amends.

4. Be transparent: Be open and honest with yourself and others. Share your thoughts and feelings, and be willing to listen to others.

5. Lead by example: Set an example for others by being true to your values and beliefs. Be consistent in your actions and words.

6. Align with your organization's values: Make sure your values align with your organization's mission and values. This will help you stay motivated and committed to your work.

7. Get feedback: Ask for feedback from your colleagues and superiors. This will help you identify areas to improve and become more congruent.

Write down these seven tips, put them on your desk and review them every day. Keep them front and center because becoming a more harmonious and congruent leader will produce more effective team players. I guarantee it!

Chapter 8

Alignment: Harmonizing Efforts for Collective Success

"Trust starts with trustworthy leadership. It must be built into the corporate culture." – Barbara Brooks Kimmell, Founder of Trust Across America-Trust Across the World

Key Six...Alignment: Ensuring that individuals' and teams' actions, goals, and efforts are coordinated and synchronized toward common objectives. A leader fosters alignment by clearly communicating expectations, providing direction, and facilitating collaboration and teamwork.

My favorite thing to do when working with my clients is to help them align their team with the vision and goals collectively to accelerate growth. Whenever you bring together a group of people, there is always potential for misalignment. Getting everyone to have a voice but eventually agree to a forward direction can be difficult. You want each stakeholder to be respectfully heard, embrace change, and work collaboratively with others to build a high-performing team or partnership.

Transparent leaders can lead great companies and achieve great results because, over time, they've built solid relationships and set their teams up for success. You can develop yourself or your team into passionate, purpose-driven leaders who wake up daily focused on excellence and bringing their A-game by providing opportunities for them to align.

When leaders take on the responsibility to compel their team to take collective action toward a desirable outcome, they reduce friction and the time it takes to accelerate results. Give your team a clear problem to solve, and watch how fast they solve it! Specify goals in advance so that interactions can be aligned with them and the knowledge gained through interactions can be selected and applied to problem-solving.

You can provide tools and facilitation for teams, board members, and partners (whether newly formed or existing) so that each stakeholder is respectfully heard, embraces change, and works collaboratively with others to build a high-performing team or partnership. The leader's role is to ensure that the actions, goals, and efforts of individual teams are coordinated and synchronized toward common objectives. If not you, then who?

Alignment is any leader's cornerstone of success. It supports collaboration, synergy, and cohesiveness. Achieving alignment can be challenging in the intricate web of human interaction. It requires adeptly navigating diverse perspectives, ensuring inclusiveness, steering individuals toward a shared vision, and motivating them to embrace change while pursuing excellence. Everyone's contribution matters.

Visionary leaders, often referred to as Transparent leaders, possess the remarkable ability to steer an organization toward greatness through alignment. Individual achievements do not merely define their success but the strength of the relationships they cultivate and the cohesive teams they build. By laying the groundwork and setting their team up for success, they empower themselves and their teams to win together and navigate challenges with agility and precision. Alignment ensures that every interaction contributes to problem-solving and facilitates the application of acquired knowledge towards achieving shared objectives.

A lack of alignment will negatively impact communication, productivity, efficiency, opportunities for collaboration, conflict resolution, engagement, change management, decision-making, and ultimately, customer satisfaction and loyalty. Lack of alignment stunts growth, period. With alignment, it is possible to accelerate growth and gain major traction. No great leader will argue otherwise.

There are several tools and strategies that will help you get your team aligned and pave the path to success. Great leaders start with a comprehensive team alignment process with an outside facilitator so they can participate as a team player. Having an unbiased outside facilitator lays the foundation for cohesive collaboration and propels teams toward monumental achievements.

So, what's in your toolbox? Below are three tools that I recommend to my clients that work! If this is your first time working with these tools, I recommend that you roll them out in the order listed below to get maximum results and buy-in. You will see as you continue that they build upon each other.

1: Team Alignment

When organizations build a strategy to achieve peak performance, they usually focus on training reps to increase sales or provide better service, implementing more streamlined processes, and hiring the right people. However, one key factor they fail to focus on is team alignment. So, what is team alignment, and why is it such a critical component to achieving peak performance in any organization?

Alignment is when the entire organization is in sync with the company vision, strategic plan, rules of the game, and there are clear expectations of roles and responsibilities. Team alignment sets expectations, solidifies relationships, and creates raving fans internally. This is the key to a high-performing culture. It is critical to achieving peak performance because it instills ownership and accountability while eliminating conflict. It links the organization's goals with team goals and creates consistency between objectives and plans. Most importantly, it instills transparency and develops trust within an organization. The outcome is clarity, transparency, common goals, commitment, and a strong culture.

The purpose of team alignment is to provide direction and focus to your team while helping them build a plan of action consistent with the organization's goals. Many CEOs, executives, and managers utilize this tool to overcome obstacles within their team and manage change. It allows them to confront their challenges and turn them into opportunities by providing an opportunity for dialogue about important issues and decisions. As a result, there is genuine buy-in around important decisions, even if there is initial disagreement because a facilitator can ensure that all opinions and ideas are brought to the table and considered. The team can achieve the clarity needed to succeed in their role.

In his book, author Patrick Lencioni states the Five Dysfunctions of a Team are:

1. Absence of Trust

2. Fear of Conflict
3. Lack of Commitment
4. Avoidance of Accountability
5. Inattention to Results

If any of these dysfunctions are lurking within your organization and keeping you from achieving peak performance, you need a team alignment ASAP! And if you have not heard of Lencioni's book, order a copy stat!

I recommend hiring an outside facilitator for the first one to understand how it is done and then consider whether you want to model the process bi-annually. Facilitation requires a unique skill set that brings an unbiased approach and outside perspective to a team alignment day. You need someone who has the skills to quickly build trust among the team, can pivot and think fast on their feet.

A well-facilitated meeting or summit will uncover out-of-the-box ideas and many times previously unknown truths about your company in a safe, collaborative environment where participants are engaged and focused on successful outcomes and plans.

#2: 90-Day Planning for Strategic Execution

In the fast-paced business world, executing a strategic plan requires more than a long-term vision; it demands actionable steps and measurable milestones. One practical approach is to develop a 13-week Action Plan, aligning with the quarterly goals set for the organization or the personal goals set for the individual. By breaking down annual goals and targets into manageable quarterly objectives and weekly action plans, leaders can ensure alignment, track progress, and develop a culture of accountability while setting their team up for success.

Two weeks before the next quarter begins is the opportune moment to rally teams and ensure alignment with annual targets. Quarterly goals and milestones serve as pivotal checkpoints to ensure you are on track to hit your yearly goals. Achieving these milestones keeps your business on course with its strategic direction, enhances profitability, and boosts team performance. By setting clear objectives for each quarter, leaders lay the groundwork for success and empower their teams to excel, minimize distractions, and eliminate confusion.

To effectively execute the 90-day plan, leaders can follow a structured approach:

1. 90-Day Goals - Begin by clarifying the end goal and assessing progress towards annual targets. Identify the gaps between current accomplishments and the desired outcomes for the next quarter. Break down these quarterly goals into monthly goals over a three month period.

2. Strategies - Determine the strategies to drive progress towards the monthly goals. Strategies are broader and focus on the overall direction of a

project, organization, or initiative. The purpose of a strategy is to set a clear vision and outline the path to reach a specific goal or objective by the end of the month or quarter.

For example: Cross- sell more products, improve customer service, elevate your brand, target a younger audience, revisit pricing strategies. Reflect on past successes and consider what you should keep doing and what you should stop doing. Be careful how many you choose to implement over a 90-day period. It is better to choose fewer and commit your resources to those few than to choose many and not have the resources to execute any of them well. The right number of strategies depending on the size of your team is usually 2-3 in any given department or business. If you choose three, for example, you can roll one out each month.

3. Activities or Tactics - Specify the activities that need to take place weekly to achieve the monthly targets. A tactic is a specific action or method used to achieve a short-term goal within the context of a

broader strategy. It is the "how-to" of executing the strategy. For example: Make a list of high net products or services to cross-sell, identify three potential new customers and set up a meeting with them, develop a survey to determine action steps to improve customer service, post five additional posts per week on social media to elevate the brand.

4. Timeline - Establish a logical timeline for executing activities and meeting monthly targets. Define the frequency and duration of each task, ensuring a systematic approach towards goal attainment. Utilize a one-page sheet with a 13-week timeline to track progress and maintain focus.

5. Responsibilities - Clearly define who is responsible for executing each activity. Whether it's individual members or specific departments, assign accountability and communicate expectations promptly. Support team members in incorporating their assigned tasks into their 90-day Action Plans, fostering a culture of ownership and collaboration.

Developing a comprehensive 90-day Action Plan requires discipline and commitment. Leaders must prioritize allocating creative time for teams to craft their plans so they can encourage cultures of transparency, performance, and accountability. By investing just two hours in this strategic exercise, your team will be capable of achieving remarkable results. It's not about complexity; instead, it's about embracing discipline and empowering teams to excel. I love setting my team up for success!

The 90-day planning approach offers a practical and effective strategy for translating long-term goals into actionable steps. You can navigate complexities with clarity and precision by breaking down annual targets into quarterly objectives. Through disciplined execution, you can help others maximize performance, drive innovation, and propel the organization toward greatness. So, are you ready to invest in your team's success and set your company on the path to excellence? Don't let the fact that you have never done it before stop you. It doesn't have to be perfect; you just have to get started. Your team will thank you for taking the time to help them see how they can reach their goals for the quarter, and you will stand out as a leader who cares about others' success.

#3: Group Coaching

When leaders invest in their people, their people invest in them. According to Gallup, a well-known research and analytics company that has conducted surveys on engagement and trust in the workplace, the percentage of employees who trust their boss tends to be around 30% to 40% globally, and half quit their jobs because they can't get along with their boss. Multiple studies and surveys have consistently shown that poor leadership or dissatisfaction with management is a significant factor in turnover.

The good news is that group coaching is an effective leadership tool that can help overcome the challenges of team engagement, alignment, retention, communication, and lack of trust.

Here are six compelling reasons why group coaching is the quintessential tool for developing team members, fostering engagement, and enhancing retention:

1. Build Trust - Trust is the bedrock of any successful team or organization. Group coaching facilitates the cultivation of transparency and accountability, fostering an environment where hidden agendas are not tolerated in favor of open and honest communication. Your team will transform, viewing themselves as integral parts of a more extensive agenda and cohesive team dedicated to advancing company initiatives. This shift in perspective breaks down barriers and empowers leaders to instill similar beliefs within their respective teams creating cohesion.

2. Strategic Focus - Group coaching eliminates personal agendas by leveraging the expertise of

external coaches who provide impartial perspectives. Consequently, discussions and communications are strategically aligned with the pillars of the company's strategic plan. By focusing on overarching goals and objectives, leaders can steer their teams toward collective success with clarity and purpose.

3. Cross Collaboration - Leadership sets the tone for collaboration within an organization. Through group coaching, leaders exemplify cross-departmental collaboration, inspiring their teams to emulate similar behaviors. By encouraging the exploration of opportunities for interdepartmental engagement, group coaching transcends traditional silos, paving the way for collaborative projects that harness the collective talents of multiple departments.

4. Avoid Duplication - Group coaching is a platform for identifying and capitalizing on opportunities to share resources and best practices. By creating an environment for knowledge exchange and

collaboration, leaders can avoid unnecessary duplication of efforts, optimizing efficiency and productivity across the organization.

5. Foster Forward-Thinking Attitudes - Regular group coaching sessions foster a forward-thinking mindset among leaders, facilitating paradigm shifts in collective thinking. By focusing discussions on solutions and innovative approaches, leaders are empowered to navigate challenges with resilience and creativity, driving continuous improvement and growth.

6. Promotes Fun and Cohesion - Group coaching injects an element of camaraderie and enjoyment into leadership and team development, resulting in cohesion and friendly competition among peers. Leaders cultivate a sense of belonging and mutual support by engaging in productive interactions within a supportive group setting, which they can then extend to their respective teams.

So, here's how group coaching works.

Groups of 4-6 meet weekly for an hour, virtually or in person. All group coaching sessions are led by an executive coach who steers the agenda. The first 30 minutes are focused on strategy, best practices, and cross-departmental collaboration. The second 30 minutes are spent understanding behavior and communication styles including 10 minutes of leadership development training.

A team assessment is administered before you begin the program and at quarterly intervals to measure the effectiveness of the group coaching. This allows the team to assess themselves before the program starts and requires them to continue to evaluate their effectiveness. Additionally, key performance indicators such as productivity, engagement, and retention are tracked to ensure measurable progress and reviewed at the beginning of each group coaching session.

In today's dynamic and competitive business landscape, engagement, trust, and collaboration are non-negotiable prerequisites for success. Group coaching is a transformative tool for cultivating these essential attributes, empowering leaders to drive organizational growth and foster a culture of excellence. By embracing group coaching as a systemic approach to leadership development, organizations can embark on a journey from good to great, transforming their cultures and achieving sustained success. With a combination of team alignment, 90 day planning, and group coaching, organizations and their leaders can unleash the full potential of their teams, foster innovation, and achieve lasting success.

People today seek more than donuts, a cool-looking office, and flexibility. They demand integrity among leaders and team members, mentorship, and a culture that demands a forward-thinking, collaborative, and creative learning environment. Great leaders take on the responsibility to interact more and facilitate more engagement and interaction among their teams so they can align, build trust, and leverage resources. This will enable you to create a culture that follows your lead, resulting in productivity increases, engagement, and retention. You will be able to attract top performers who are driven by results and are looking for a customized approach to help them hit their targets.

Establishing customized cross-functional group coaching programs will position you as an innovative and creative leader who provides interactive alternatives to the canned one-size-fits-all leadership development workshops and weekly team meetings. Transforming your culture is a system-wide approach that starts at the top.

With team alignment, 90-day planning, and group coaching your team will want to talk about the future, embrace long-term planning, share ideas, and show up!   Create transparent environments through alignment, encourage communication, and help your team grow while eliminating toxicity that will destroy your culture.

Chapter 9

Measurement - Guiding Success through Data and Insight

"Effective leadership requires a commitment to continuous improvement and a willingness to embrace feedback. Measurement provides the necessary feedback loop to assess progress, identify areas for growth, and drive meaningful change. As a leader, it's essential to cultivate a culture of measurement and accountability, empowering your team to strive for excellence and achieve collective success." - Sheryl Sandberg.

Key Seven...Measurement: Systematic assessment and evaluation of progress towards goals and objectives. A leader uses relevant metrics, key performance indicators (KPIs), and feedback mechanisms to track performance, identify areas for improvement, and make informed decisions to drive success.

So, what is the measurement tool in your business and among your team? Most people can accept the thinking behind it, but what measurements do you have in place to determine improvement, and who is responsible for being the driving force? Do you have a Chief Accountability Officer or a Chief Performance Officer? Does each team member have a key performance indicator they are accountable for that is transparent to all team members?   How are you making decisions in the business or within your department without measuring and reviewing the key KPIs?

If you anticipate any type of massive growth and want to create a high-performing, equitable culture, this is a non-negotiable. You can't make any significant decisions in business without looking at the numbers, and your team can't hit its goals if it isn't tracking its numbers. Measurement is critical to any company when creating a vision and plan for the future that will require change, accountability, and cultural development to achieve the overall goal.

Tracking key metrics ensures goals are on track, assists in the formulation and execution of your team's long and short-term strategies, ensures team alignment, instills a culture of transparency and fairness within the organization, and ensures open and honest communication throughout the organization.

There will be resistance and fear of transparency in the numbers. For this reason, you must communicate the value and share your intent to set your team and the company up for success. It's common for people to perceive this as a negative, making them feel that they are being audited and watched at all times in fear of losing their jobs. Communicate the upside. Let them know this evens the playing field and prevents others from making decisions based on how they feel and how this will work in their favor providing them goals, purpose and most importantly, clarity in the expectations for their role.

Lack of measurement in any business will result in a lack of clarity and direction, ineffective decision-making, difficulty in performance evaluation, inefficient resource allocation, inconsistent quality, limited accountability, challenges in strategic planning, and missed opportunities for improvement. The list goes on and on. I once worked with a client who had been in business for 25 years and didn't know how to determine his profit margin. If you don't know your profit margin, you don't know how or if you need to improve it. Numbers tell a story. Measurement establishes transparency and accountability throughout the entire organization, sets expectations and clearly, without doubt, identifies areas of opportunity for growth.

Measurement is the linchpin of effective leadership, providing a systematic framework for assessing progress, identifying areas for improvement, and driving organizational success. By strategically utilizing relevant metrics, key performance indicators (KPIs), and feedback mechanisms, leaders gain invaluable insights into their teams' and businesses' health and performance. In this chapter, we delve into the critical role of measurement in fostering accountability, transparency, and a culture of high performance.

The Significance of Measurement

You can't improve what you don't measure. This old adage encapsulates the essence of measurement in both personal and professional contexts. Just as individuals track their weight loss progress or monitor a child's growth, businesses must rely on concrete metrics to gauge performance and track progress toward their goals. Yet, despite its logical appeal, many organizations need to improve when implementing effective measurement practices.

Establishing Accountability and Transparency

Effective measurement necessitates clear accountability and transparency throughout the organization. Leaders must designate individuals responsible for tracking key metrics and communicate performance expectations transparently. This fosters a culture of accountability where team members take ownership of their responsibilities and strive for excellence. Organizations can align their teams toward common goals and drive collective success by establishing clear performance metrics and expectations.

Overcoming Resistance and Fostering Growth

Resistance to measurement often stems from fears of transparency and scrutiny. To overcome this resistance, leaders can communicate the purpose and benefits of measurement as tools for setting their team up for success while driving performance and growth. By framing measurement initiatives as supportive mechanisms for organizational success, leaders can mitigate fears and gain buy-in from team members. It's crucial to emphasize that measurement is not about surveillance but rather empowering individuals and the organization to achieve their full potential.

Core Metrics for Success

Simplicity is vital to navigating the vast landscape of metrics. Rather than overwhelming teams with many data points, focus on a concise set of core metrics that drive value and stability. For CEOs and executive teams, I recommend starting with six key metrics:

1. Pipeline - Often overlooked at the executive level, the pipeline is a vital indicator of future revenue streams. Organizations can make informed decisions about marketing investments and revenue projections by monitoring leads, conversion rates, and overall pipeline health.

2. Revenue - The lifeblood of any business, revenue is a fundamental metric for assessing financial health and growth trajectories.

3. Revenue Concentration - This is the total amount of your total revenue that is dependent on one client or a subset of clients. Understanding revenue

concentration helps mitigate risk by identifying over-reliance on specific clients or revenue streams. You want your revenue concentration to be balanced.

4. Revenue Churn - This is the rate at which monthly recurring revenue is lost. Churn rates provide insights into customer satisfaction and retention, guiding efforts to enhance customer experience and loyalty.

5. Team Engagement - A highly engaged team is correlated with increased productivity, retention, and overall organizational success.

6. EBITDA (Burn Rate) - Earnings Before Interest, Taxes, Depreciation and Amortization. EBITDA offers insights into operational efficiency and sustainability, guiding strategic financial decisions and resource allocation.

Measurement is not merely a matter of tracking numbers; it drives organizational performance and success. By embracing measurement as a catalyst for accountability, transparency, and continuous improvement, leaders can empower their teams to achieve remarkable results. Through the strategic selection of core metrics and clear communication of expectations, organizations can navigate complexity with clarity and precision, setting the stage for sustained growth and excellence. So, are you ready to unlock the full potential of your team and organization through strategic measurement?

A lack of measurement in the workplace can have significant negative impacts on individuals, teams, and organizations:

1. **Decreased Performance**: Without the numbers, individuals may lack clarity about their roles, responsibilities, and expectations. This ambiguity can lead to confusion, duplication of efforts, and ultimately decreased performance and productivity.

2. **Missed Deadlines and Goals**: When individuals or teams are not held accountable to their numbers, actions and expected outcomes,

there is a higher likelihood of missed deadlines and failure to achieve goals. Without accountability mechanisms like key performance indicators, underperformance may have no consequences, leading to a lack of urgency and commitment to meeting objectives.

3. **Diminished Trust and Morale**: A lack of measurement erodes trust among team members and between employees and management. When individuals perceive that others are not held accountable, it can lead to resentment, frustration, and unfairness. This can damage team cohesion and morale.

4. **Increased Conflict**: Without measurement, misunderstandings, conflicts, and disagreements may arise more frequently within teams and across departments. When individuals feel that others are not fulfilling their responsibilities or are not being held to the same standards, tension and conflict can occur in the workplace. The numbers take the focus off how someone feels and allow you to deal with the facts when discussing performance.

5. **Decreased Innovation and Creativity**: In an environment lacking accountability, individuals may be less motivated to take initiative, share ideas, or propose innovative solutions. Fear of failure or reprisal may prevent team members from taking risks or thinking outside the box, stifling creativity and innovation. You can avoid this by instilling proper measurement.

6. **Risk of Errors and Compliance Issues**: Without measurement, there is a higher risk of errors, mistakes, and compliance issues within organizations. When individuals are not given clear, measurables, there may be a lack of oversight and quality control, leading to costly errors or breaches of regulations.

7. **Negative Organizational Culture**: A lack of measurables can contribute to a toxic organizational culture characterized by blame-shifting and finger-pointing. Measurables help you make others feel that they are being treated fairly. A lack of measurement can undermine teamwork, collaboration, and trust,

making it difficult for the organization to achieve its goals.

8. **Loss of Reputation and Credibility**: Organizations that fail to hold their teams accountable for their performance may suffer damage to their reputation and credibility. Leaders must establish and advocate for precise accountability mechanisms and hold individuals accountable for their actions and outcomes to achieve high performance.

Be consciously aware of your level of measurement among your team and within your entire organization. It takes a great level of vulnerability and congruence to create a culture where decisions are made based on data because leaders have to also be transparent and accountable to their key performance indicators to garner support for this level of transparency and accountability. Have the courage to instill key performance indicators throughout, review them weekly and watch your team soar! Some team members will not respond positively and may even deselect themselves from continuing to be part of your team. That's ok. Remember, how you show up is how everything and everyone shows up around you. A rising tide raises all ships.

Chapter 10

The Kaizen Principle: Constant & Neverending Improvement

"I learned to always take on things I'd never done before. Growth and comfort do not coexist."
- Ginni Rometty (Executive Chairman, IBM)

When I started life as an entrepreneur in 2005, I learned about the Kaizen Principle, which has been part of my daily grind ever since. I wake up and ask myself daily, what can I learn today to enrich my life, grow my business, and get uncomfortable?

The Kaizen Principle underscores the importance of constant and never-ending improvement. As a leader, fostering a culture of continual growth and development within your team is imperative. It's a responsibility to the organization, to oneself, and the world to continuously learn, see things through a different lens, and teach others to do the same if you want to create an impact. If you are comfortable, you are status quo. Great leaders are not status quo; they help others grow both professionally and personally while developing themselves. The best way to teach the Kaizen Principle is to model the behavior and ask yourself daily what you will do to improve. What will you do to ensure you pick up just one new golden nugget each day?

I have been reading business and personal development books since 2005. I have not read a single fictional book since then. I commit to reading or listening to two books per month, and I share my lessons with others. Sometimes, I let people know I have just read the book and encourage them to purchase it themselves or gift it to them. If it resonates, someone will take action. If you have influence, more will take action. My thirst for learning allows me to mentor others with more than my thoughts, opinions, and experience. The point is that your input is your output. What you absorb and digest is what you convey, think, and it determines how you show up for others.

I stopped listening to the news in 2007. I had recently left my lobbying position at the law firm and just couldn't take the banter over the politics anymore, the deaths reported, and the devastating acts of mother nature that claimed lives. It changed my life. You would be amazed at how eliminating the news changes your attitude. Most people don't even realize how much the news impacts their thinking, mood, and ability to change the world. Getting rid of the background noise allowed me to read more, have more time to exercise, and have more time for conversation with my family.

Take note that a majority of the news is negative. Rarely is there something positive celebrated on the news. Some people will try to challenge you and say you are out of touch with the world, but are you? Ask them to audit the news for three days and report back what information they received that will make their life better. Were they joyful and hopeful when they watched the news, or did they experience sadness, fear, anger, and hopelessness? Was it a good use of time or a waste of time?

I started becoming consciously aware of my environment around 2010. Note that I didn't say 2005. I had a lot to learn between 2005 and 2010. In 2010, I realized more negative behaviors that were surrounding me and affecting me. I was frustrated with the traffic and the commute to work. I felt like everyone around me was concerned about keeping up with the Joneses. Instead of feeling like I was growing, I was dying. So, I made a change. I moved myself and my family 240 miles away to change my environment. In the same year, I stopped tolerating childhood friends who weren't good people and drained my time, energy, and drive.

You don't have to make such a drastic change but realize that you can, and only you, control your surroundings and your ability to grow. You don't have to stay stuck. That is a limiting belief that you have the power to overcome. You can change how you feel about anything. You can change your environment. You can change how you react to certain situations. If you don't feel you are living up to your potential, it is within your control and no one else's to change it. Let that sink in. It is your self-awareness and your choices that will determine your outcomes. Growth involves change and change will make you uncomfortable and that is when the magic happens. When you are uncomfortable, that is when you will notice real growth taking place.

So, do you practice the Kaizen Principle? It's never too late to do so. Determining the answer to the four questions below will start you on your journey or perhaps enhance the journey you are already on.

1. How many books will you read this year?
2. Who are the five people that you will surround yourself with that will help you grow?

3. Take inventory of what you watch on TV, your phone, or your computer. Is it draining your life or enriching your life?

4. What mentor do you want to follow this year? Will you attend their event? Invest in their course online? Watch or sign up for their daily inspiration?

Chapter 11

Your Action Plan for Impact

"Leadership is about making others better due to your presence and ensuring that impact lasts in your absence." - Sheryl Sandberg.

Becoming a transparent leader who develops a transparent culture requires a comprehensive action plan. Below are some recommendations to get you started and help you build your own action plan. Just pick three of the strategies and/or tactics listed below, implement one each month for the next 3 months, and imagine where you will be in 90 days.

1. Assessment and Alignment

   - Conduct a thorough assessment of the current culture, leadership practices, and communication processes to identify areas for improvement.

- Align your values, goals, and objectives with the Seven Essential Keys of Transparent Leadership.

2. Leadership Development

- Provide training and development opportunities for leaders and managers to enhance their understanding and application of the seven essential keys.

- Offer workshops, seminars, and coaching sessions focused on accountability, transparency, vision, and measurement.

3. Communication Strategy

- Develop a clear communication strategy emphasizing openness, clarity, and accessibility.

- Encourage leaders to communicate openly, share information transparently, and actively engage in dialogue with their team at all levels.

4. Establishing Accountability Measures

- Implement systems and processes to ensure 360-degree accountability throughout the organization.

- Define clear roles, responsibilities, and expectations for your team and hold individuals accountable for their actions, decisions, and outcomes.

5. Integrity and Ethics Training

- Provide ethics training and resources to promote honesty, sincerity, and upholding of moral principles among leaders and their teams.

- Foster a fairness, trustworthiness, and consistency culture by leading by example and reinforcing ethical behavior.

6. Transparency Initiatives

- Implement transparency initiatives such as regular town hall meetings, open-door policies, and feedback mechanisms to encourage open communication and information sharing.

- Share organizational goals, strategies, and decision-making processes with your team and provide reasons behind decisions to foster trust and understanding.

7. Vision Casting

- Develop and communicate a compelling vision for future direction and goals.

- Inspire commitment and alignment towards the vision by engaging your team in goal-setting and demonstrating how their contributions support the larger objectives.

8. Ensuring Congruence

- Ensure alignment and consistency between words, actions, and values at all levels of the organization.

- Encourage leaders to lead authentically, practice what they preach, and uphold key values in their day-to-day actions and decisions.

9. Facilitating Alignment and Collaboration

- Facilitate alignment and collaboration among individuals and teams by providing clear direction, fostering teamwork, and breaking down silos.
- Encourage cross-functional collaboration, knowledge sharing, and coordinated efforts towards common objectives.

10. Implementing Measurement and Feedback Mechanisms

- Establish relevant metrics, key performance indicators (KPIs), and feedback mechanisms to measure progress towards goals and objectives.

- Regularly review performance data, solicit feedback, and use insights to make informed decisions and drive continuous improvement.

11. Continuous Improvement

- Create a culture of continuous improvement by encouraging experimentation, learning from mistakes, and adapting strategies based on feedback and results.

- Regularly review and refine leadership practices, communication processes, and initiatives to ensure alignment with the seven essential keys of transparent leadership.

12. Recognition and Reinforcement

- Recognize and reward individuals and teams demonstrating exemplary leadership behaviors aligned with the seven essential keys.

- Reinforce the importance of accountability, integrity, transparency, vision, alignment, and measurement through ongoing communication, training, and recognition programs.

By implementing this action plan, you can cultivate a transparent culture characterized by strong leadership, open communication, shared vision, alignment, and a commitment to accountability and continuous improvement. Choose three strategies or tactics from above and get started!

Chapter 12

The Essence of Leadership

"We need to accept that we don't always make the right decisions, that we'll screw up royally sometimes. Understand that failure is not the opposite of success, it's part of success."
- Arianna Huffington (Founder & CEO, Thrive Global)

Leadership is not a fixed trait but a skill developed and honed over time. You don't have to be perfect or have all the answers. Influential leaders learn from their mistakes, admit them, pivot, and seek input from others to correct them.

We need more women in leadership. Certain traits and behaviors contribute to the effectiveness of women in leading teams:

1. **Empathy and Emotional Intelligence**: Women are often perceived as being more empathetic and

emotionally intelligent, which can help them understand the needs and motivations of team members. This ability to empathize and connect with others fosters trust, collaboration, and a supportive team environment.

2. **Communication Skills**: Women are often seen as effective communicators, adept at both listening and expressing themselves. Effective communication is crucial for articulating a shared vision, providing feedback, resolving conflicts, and keeping team members motivated and engaged.

3. **Collaborative Leadership Style**: Women are more inclined toward a collaborative leadership style, valuing input from team members and seeking consensus in decision-making processes. This approach leads to more inclusive and participatory team dynamics, where diverse perspectives are considered and respected.

4. **Resilience and Adaptability**: Women have acquired resilience and adaptability skills through navigating societal and professional challenges.

This resilience is valuable in leadership roles, particularly in fast-paced or uncertain environments, where the ability to navigate obstacles and bounce back from setbacks is essential.

5. **Diverse Perspectives**: Diversity in leadership brings diverse perspectives and problem-solving approaches to the table. Having women in leadership positions can contribute to a broader range of ideas and insights, enriching the decision-making process and enhancing innovation within teams.

6. **Empowerment of Others**: Research suggests that women leaders often prioritize the development and empowerment of their team members. By providing opportunities for growth, mentoring, and skill-building, women leaders can establish a more engaged and motivated workforce.

7. **Integrity and Ethics**: Some studies suggest that women are perceived as being more ethical

and principled in their leadership practices. This commitment to integrity and ethical behavior can build trust and credibility with team members, stakeholders, and the broader community.

There are several powerhouse companies that have been led by female CEOs who have emphasized the importance of transparency in their leadership and attributed it to their success. The following females have demonstrated how transparency in leadership can lead to greater trust, better relationships with stakeholders, and success for their companies.

1. **Mary Barra, General Motors (GM)** - Mary became the CEO of General Motors in 2014. She is known for her commitment to transparency, especially during challenging times, such as during the company's recalls. Her open communication and willingness to address issues head-on have been praised as key aspects of her leadership.

2. **Katrina Lake, Stitch Fix** - As the founder and former CEO of Stitch Fix, she emphasized

transparency in her approach to customer service and company culture, creating an environment of trust and open communication.

3. **Susan Wojcicki, You Tube** - Susan was the CEO of YouTube from 2014 to 2023. She focused on transparency with content creators, advertisers, and the public by providing regular updates on platform policies and changes, as well as hosting open forums for creators.

4. **Indra Nooyi, PepsiCo** - Indra served as the CEO of PepsiCo from 2006 to 2018. She emphasized transparency in her leadership, particularly around the company's sustainability efforts and corporate social responsibility initiatives.

As the world continues to strive for greater diversity, equity, and inclusion, acknowledging and leveraging the unique traits, skills, and behaviors that women bring to leadership roles is essential. By embracing empathy, communication, collaboration, resilience, and integrity, women leaders inspire and empower their teams to achieve greater success and drive positive change. As we move forward, let us continue to champion women in leadership and create environments where women have the opportunity to thrive and demonstrate their full leadership potential to impact future generations. They are counting on us! The world is counting on us!

I want you to step into your power and not put it on the shelf or hold back until your kids are off to school, your mom and dad are in the perfect retirement community, your brother recovers from his setback, your husband takes his foot off the gas or your friend doesn't need you anymore.

It's natural to doubt one's leadership potential or not make yourself a priority, but it's essential not to let fear, self-doubt, inconvenient times or unconventional situations hold you back. I am here to remind you that you are enough! With dedication, perseverance, and a willingness to learn, you can grow into a capable and effective leader that is unleashing your true leadership potential.

You can navigate the seasons and maintain the incredible leader that you already are or develop into the leader you are meant to be. Even if you are experiencing a setback, I want you to know that what you may be perceiving as a setback is actually setting you up for future success. Building a solid support network of mentors, colleagues, and peers can provide valuable guidance, encouragement, and perspective. Seeking leadership development opportunities, such as training programs or workshops, can also help build confidence and enhance leadership capabilities.

Leading a team is like riding a roller coaster. It can be thrilling and at times it can be terrifying. Fight through it. You are worth it. If you don't think you have what it takes, get better. Work harder on yourself than you are working in the business. Successful leaders are committed to constant and never-ending improvement.

Transparent leadership is refreshing. It allows one to be authentic. No more beating around the bush. No more hiding behind your computer. Transparent leadership spurs curiosity and innovation, a culture of learning and accountability. You can be a decision-maker, a good listener, a change agent, a mentor, a collaborator, and a motivator all at the same time. Be a transparent leader that inspires and motivates their team members by creating a compelling vision and rallying them around common goals. Lead by example and encourage personal growth and development among your team. Reward good performances and call out poor performances. Establish clear expectations and provide feedback based on predetermined criteria.

You don't have to have a magnetic personality or influence others through charm, confidence, and persuasiveness. You can earn respect with solid communication skills, by being authentic and doing the right thing!   Whether you prioritize the needs of your team above your own or adopt a hands-off approach offering your team members a high degree of autonomy, the non-negotiable is transparency. Lead with your heart, listen with two ears, and speak from experience. Blend and adapt your leadership styles based on the needs of your team and the circumstances they face so that:

❖ Challenges are solved much faster.

❖ Work relationships are more authentic.

❖ Team members trust you as their leader and are more loyal; and

❖ The organization becomes a high-performing, predictable engine.

When you implement the seven keys I shared with you in this book, future generations will feel your impact. That's how powerful you are! Whether you are the CEO, entrepreneur, a seasoned executive, a gigger or an aspiring leader, I hope this book has been helpful to you and that you are inspired to step into your power and become the influential leader that others need you to be. It's time, let's go! Join the movement.....the world is waiting!

ABOUT SHERI

Former international lobbyist and franchise executive turned business strategist and leadership coach. Before founding Business Accelerators, LLC and serving as John Mattone's Global COO, Sheri served as a franchise executive, international lobbyist, and trusted advisor to Fortune 100 companies.

As an international lobbyist working for a prominent Chicago law firm, Sheri advised CEOs and General Counsels in the medical device industry on global strategy to achieve legislative and regulatory objectives. She also played a lead role in connecting people and special interest groups adversely affected by the legislation, coaching them on how to amend or defeat the legislation by cultivating their power of influence. She successfully lobbied Congress, administration, local, state, and international governments gathering support and influencing much-needed change while managing a coalition of state lobbyists and successfully defeated 26 pieces of legislation.

As a former franchise executive for Intelligent Leadership Executive Coaching and Master Licensee for Action Coach Global, she guided her teams and coached clients to achieve an increase in revenue and profit through planning, process design, leadership development, and training. She is the glue that holds any team together. Sheri puts her heart and soul into anything she builds. Even in times of adversity she always takes the high road and puts her best foot forward.

Sheri is passionate about scaling business through people. She has helped companies increase their revenue by 46% in profit by 61% by helping leaders level up and coaching high performers to find their moral compass, lead with a big heart, and develop a solid conviction to do the right thing. She's a visionary who sees beyond the horizon, painting a vivid picture of what could be. But her vision isn't confined to dreams—it's grounded in action. She possesses the rare ability of a visionary to turn vision into reality through execution. She has the unique ability to seamlessly integrate strategy, people, and purpose. Her leadership isn't fragmented; it's holistic.

Renowned for her engaging and thought provoking speaking and coaching style, Sheri has left a lasting impact on leaders worldwide. From startups to multinational corporations, non-profits, government departments, and companies seek Sheri's expertise to uncover organizational challenges and chart a transformative course for business and leadership success.

For nearly 20 years, Sheri has coached over 1000 entrepreneur CEOs and executives and their teams to become the best version of themselves and become leaders that others want to follow while building cultures that attract and retain team members. Her friends and colleagues describe her as driven, fun, intelligent, and loyal. Leading executives and their teams to their highest potential is her personal and professional mission.

She empowers her clients to achieve personal growth, ongoing professional development business and organizational success.

Approachable, educational, and accessible, Sheri connects with entrepreneurs and seasoned leaders alike. In her upcoming book, Transparent Leadership – 7 Keys to Unlock Your True Leadership Potential, Sheri delves into the essential elements for fostering a truly transparent culture. Drawing from personal experiences, she shares real-life examples of businesses and leaders she has guided to transformation.

B.S. Political Science

Certified Master Executive Coach with John Mattone Global, Inc

Certified Business Coach & Executive Coach with Action Coach Global

Certified Executive Coach, ACTP, ICF Accredited Coach Training Program, Center for Executive Coaching

Certified Professional Behavior Analyst, TTI Success Insights

To follow me for free leadership tips and resources
or book me as a speaker for your next event, scan
the QR code below.

Made in United States
Troutdale, OR
07/20/2024

21421727R00080